A Day in the Life: Grassland Animals

Ostrich

Louise Spilsbury

Heinemann
LIBRARY

Chicago, Illinois

www.heinemannraintree.com
Visit our website to find out more information about Heinemann-Raintree books.

To order:
☎ Phone 888-454-2279
▭ Visit www.heinemannraintree.com
to browse our catalog and order online.

©2011 Heinemann Library
an imprint of Capstone Global Library, LLC
Chicago, Illinois

Edited by Dan Nunn, Rebecca Rissman, Catherine Veitch, and Nancy Dickmann
Designed by Philippa Jenkins
Picture research by Mica Brancic
Originated by Capstone Global Library
Printed and bound in China by South China Printing Company Ltd

14 13 12 11 10
10 9 8 7 6 5 4 3 2 1

Library of Congress Cataloging-in-Publication Data
Spilsbury, Louise.
  Ostrich / Louise Spilsbury.
    p. cm. — (A day in the life. Grassland animals)
  Includes bibliographical references and index.
  ISBN 978-1-4329-4730-9 (hc) — ISBN 978-1-4329-4740-8 (pb) 1. Ostriches—Juvenile literature. I. Title.
  QL696.S9S65 2011
  598.5'24—dc22   2010017848

Acknowledgments
We would like to thank the following for permission to reproduce photographs: Alamy pp. 6 (© Robert Fried), 10 (© MNS Photo), 12 (© Imagebroker/Bernd Zoller), 13 (© Lana Sundman), 19 (© Juniors Bildarchiv); Ardea p. 16 (© J. L. Mason); FLPA p. 17 (Sunset); iStockphoto p. 23 cheetah (© BostjanT); Nature Picture Library p. 22 (© Tony Heald); Shutterstock pp. 4 (© Urosr), 5 (© Eric Isselée), 7, 23 female, 23 male (© Four Oaks), 9, 23 grassland (© Mdd), 11 (© Mogens Trolle), 14 (© Smeyf), 15 (© John Carnemolla), 18, 23 mongoose (© Palko72), 20 (© Gallofoto), 21 (© Hallam Creations), 23 hyena (© Antonio Jorge Nunes), 23 insect (© kd2).

Cover photograph of a close-up portrait of an ostrich reproduced with permission of Shutterstock (© Petr Vaclavek). Back cover photographs of (left) an ostrich with eggs reproduced with permission of Shutterstock (© Eric Isselée) and (right) ostrich chicks reproduced with permission of FLPA (Sunset).

We would like to thank Michael Bright for his invaluable help in the preparation of this book.

The author would like to dedicate this book to her nephew and niece, Ben and Amelie: "I wrote these books for animal lovers like you. I hope you enjoy them". Aunty Louise.

Every effort has been made to contact copyright holders of material reproduced in this book. Any omissions will be rectified in subsequent printings if notice is given to the publisher.

Contents

Some words are in bold, **like this**. You can find out what they mean by looking in the glossary.

What Is an Ostrich?

An ostrich is a big bird that has wings but cannot fly.

The ostrich is the largest bird in the world.

Ostriches lay bigger eggs than any other bird.

An ostrich egg is as big as a medium-sized melon!

What Do Ostriches Look Like?

Ostriches have a long neck and legs, and are taller than most men.

They have small heads, but their eyes are as big as baseballs!

Ostriches have long fluffy feathers on their back and wings.

Males have black and white feathers, and **females** have mostly brown feathers.

Where Do Ostriches Live?

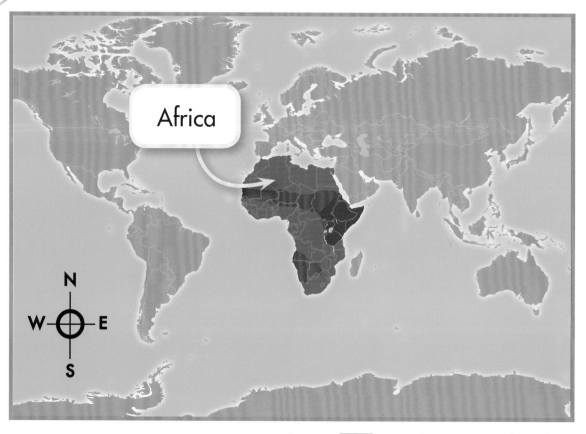

Africa

key: = where ostriches live

Ostriches live in parts of central and southern Africa.

They mostly live in places called **grasslands**.

In these grasslands the land is mostly covered in grasses.

Most days it is hot and dry, but in some months it rains a lot.

What Do Ostriches Do During the Day?

In the mornings and afternoons, ostriches feed.

On days when it gets very hot, they rest in the middle of the day.

Sometimes ostriches rub their bodies in dust.

This helps to keep their feathers in good shape.

What Do Ostriches Eat?

food

Ostriches eat grasses and other plants, and sometimes **insects** too.

Ostriches only swallow when they have a big lump of food in their throat!

Ostriches also eat sand and small stones.

These help the birds grind up the food that they swallow.

How Do Ostriches Move?

In the day, ostriches usually walk around slowly.

They hold their heads up high to look out for danger.

Ostriches cannot fly, but they can run quickly if they spot trouble.

Ostriches can run twice as fast as a human!

Where Do Ostriches Lay Eggs?

egg

Female ostriches lay their eggs together in a shared nest.

Females keep eggs warm and safe during the day, and **males** take over at night.

Ostrich chicks are striped so they are hard to see among the grasses in the day.

When it is hot they hide from the sun under their parents' wings.

Which Animals Hunt Ostriches?

mongoose

Mongooses and some other animals eat ostrich eggs and chicks.

Ostrich parents watch their eggs and chicks carefully to keep them safe.

Cheetahs, lions, leopards, wild dogs, and **hyenas** hunt adult ostriches.

Ostriches escape by running away or kicking these animals with their strong legs!

What Do Ostriches Do at Night?

Ostriches sleep at night.

They sleep sitting down on the ground.

At night it can get cold in the **grasslands** where ostriches live.

To keep warm, an ostrich wraps its wings around itself like a blanket!

Ostrich Body Map

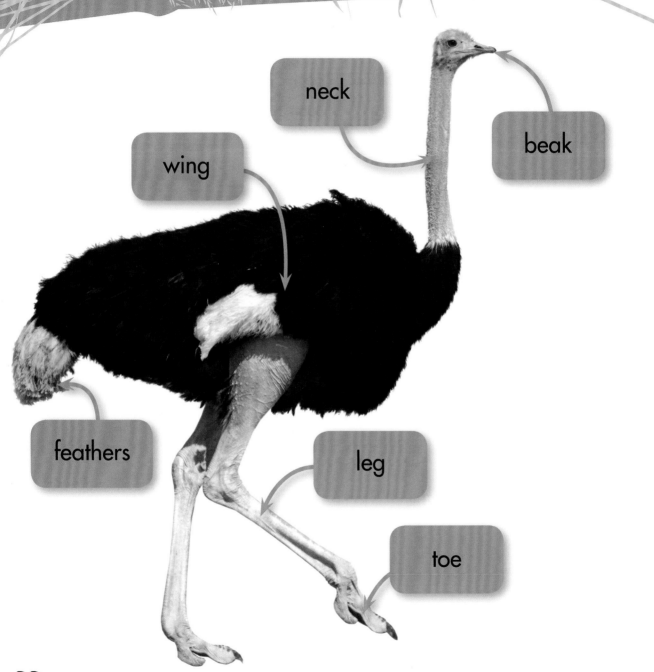

neck

beak

wing

feathers

leg

toe

Glossary

 **cheetah** large, spotted wild cat. A cheetah lives in Africa.

 **female** animal that can become a mother when it is grown up

 **grassland** land where mostly grasses grow

 **hyena** wild animal that mostly lives in grasslands in Africa. It looks like a dog.

 **insect** small animal with six legs. Ants, beetles, and bees are insects.

 **male** animal that can become a father when it is grown up

 **mongoose** wild animal that lives in Asia and Africa. It looks like a weasel.

Find Out More

Books

Maynard, Thane. *Ostriches (New Naturebooks)*. Mankato, MN: Child's World, 2006.

Stout, Frankie. *Ostriches: Nature's Biggest Birds (Things With Wings)*. New York: PowerKids Press, 2008.

Websites

http://animals.nationalgeographic.com/animals/birds/ostrich.html

http://www.bbc.co.uk/nature/species/Ostrich

Index